PART 2

> **Describe a situation when someone that you didn't know helped you.**
>
> **You should say:**
>
> > **what the situation was**
> > **when and where it happened**
> > **how the person helped you**
>
> **and explain how you felt in that situation**

You will have to talk about the topic for 1 to 2 minutes.

You have 1 minute to think about what you are going to say.

You can make some notes to help you if you wish.

TASK CARD 2

PART 2

> **Describe a day out that you remember when you went out with friends.**
>
> > **You should say:**
> >
> > > **who the friends were**
> > > **where you went**
> > > **what you did**
>
> **and explain why you remember that day out so well**

You will have to talk about the topic for 1 to 2 minutes.

You have 1 minute to think about what you are going to say.

You can make some notes to help you if you wish.

Speaking Test Preparation Pack for

IELTS

University of Cambridge ESOL Examinations
1 Hills Road
Cambridge
CB1 2EU
UK

www.CambridgeESOL.org

© UCLES 2010

First published 2010

Project managed by Cambridge Publishing Management Ltd

Printed in the United Kingdom by Océ (UK) Ltd

ISBN 978-1-906438-86-9

Contents

Introduction

This *Speaking Test Preparation Pack for IELTS* has been specially created to help you to prepare your students for the Speaking test of the International English Language Testing System (IELTS). Written by experienced IELTS Speaking test examiners, it consists of:

- a book containing comprehensive Teacher's Notes and a set of nine Student Worksheets that provide detailed practice for all parts of the IELTS Speaking test
- candidate task cards to allow you and your students to practise with realistic exam materials
- a DVD showing real students taking a Speaking test to give your students a clear idea of what to expect on the day.

The Student Worksheets can be photocopied to use in class, or printed from the files on the DVD if you prefer. They cover the three parts of the Speaking test in detail and contain a variety of exercises and discussion tasks using the DVD. There are two worksheets for each of the three parts of the test and three more general worksheets based on the test as a whole.

The Teacher's Notes for each worksheet explain how to conduct each activity, and provide answers to and commentary on the various exercises.

The DVD contains a recording of one complete IELTS Speaking test, along with the Student Worksheets and candidate task cards. As well as the complete test, the three parts of the test are included separately for ease of use. The timing on each of the three parts starts at 00.00. The timings given in the Teacher's Notes correspond to the timings on the separate parts of the DVD, indicating which specific section you should play for the exercises on the Student Worksheets.

We hope you enjoy using the *Speaking Test Preparation Pack for IELTS* and wish your students every success when they take the test.

■ Aims of the DVD and worksheets

- to raise students' awareness of the format of the IELTS Speaking test
- to focus students' attention on techniques that will improve their performance
- to provide opportunities for students to practise the language used in the different parts of the test.

Please note:

The DVD and worksheets are not intended as a forum for discussing grades. Although in certain questions we are asking students to look at the candidates' performance, it is with a view to improving their own performance and not for them to grade the candidates on the DVD.

The IELTS Speaking test on the DVD has been produced for teaching purposes only and is not a live exam. There are, therefore, no grades available.

Cambridge ESOL

IELTS Speaking test
Teacher's Notes

This worksheet focuses on general information about the IELTS Speaking test, and introduces students to the format of the test.

Time needed: 25 minutes

■ Task One: General information about the IELTS Speaking test
(10 minutes)

Ask the students to fill in the missing information about the IELTS Speaking test in pairs.

Check answers.

Answers (in bold)

1. The length of the test is **11–14** minutes.

2. The normal format is **one** candidate/s and **one** examiner/s.

3. There are **three** parts to the test.

4. The Speaking test is worth **25**% of the whole IELTS test.

■ Task Two: Match the two
(15 minutes)

Ask the students to match the information about what happens in each part of the Speaking test in pairs.

Check answers.

Answers

A	B
Part 1 lasts for	4–5 minutes
In Part 1, the examiner	greets the candidate and asks questions selected from familiar topics
In Part 1, the candidate	gives personal information
Part 2 lasts for	3–4 minutes
In Part 2, the examiner	gives the candidates a topic to speak about and asks a rounding-off question
In Part 2, the candidate	speaks for 1–2 minutes on a topic related to their experience
Part 3 lasts for	4–5 minutes
In Part 3, the examiner	leads a general discussion of a more abstract nature connected to the Part 2 topic
In Part 3, the candidate	gives general views and opinions on the topic

IELTS Speaking test
Teacher's Notes

This worksheet is based on the introductory section of Part 1 of the IELTS Speaking test. The introductory frame of Part 1 is centred around general information on the place where candidates live, or on work/study. The questions are designed to elicit a range of tenses. Students can prepare to some extent for this part, and this is designed to put them at ease at the start of the test. The introductory frame will usually take about one minute or slightly longer. The timing for the whole of Part 1 is four to five minutes.

Time needed: 1 hour (1 hour 10 minutes with Optional activity)

■ Task One: Vocabulary brainstorm (5 minutes)

Ask the students to brainstorm useful vocabulary and phrases related to where they live. The topic of 'Where you live' could be related to their home as well as to their town/city. It would be a good idea to brainstorm vocabulary and phrases for this as well. For further practice, students could create questions about their house/apartment and practise asking and answering them in pairs as in **Task Six** below.

■ Task Two: Questions and answers (15 minutes)

1. Tell the students to work with a partner and ask and answer the questions in turn.

   • What do you like most about your home town/city? [Why?]

   • Is your home town/city a popular place for tourists to visit? [Why/Why not?]

   • Has your home town/city changed much in recent years? [How?]

2. Play the introductory sections for both candidates on the DVD (Inmi: 00.00–01.52; Leonardo: 00.00–01.43). Ask the students to discuss in pairs how their answers were different from Inmi's and Leonardo's in terms of the length and detail.

Encourage the students to think about how well they answered the questions, and how they feel about the answers from the candidates on the DVD.

■ Task Three: Watch and listen (15 minutes)

1. Play this part of the DVD again and ask the students to make notes in the table on their worksheet. Ask the students to compare their notes with other students in the group and then go through the answers with them.

Answers

What does Inmi say about ...	What does Leonardo say about ...
what she likes most about Seoul? *There are lots of exciting places such as theatres.*	what he likes most about Venice? *It is one of the most beautiful places in the world, particularly the quieter corners.*
Seoul's popularity with tourists? *It is very popular because of the antique palaces.*	Venice's popularity with tourists? *Leonardo answers this under question 1, when he says how popular Venice is with tourists. The interlocutor therefore omits this question.*
whether it has changed recently? *Yes. Public transport is more convenient.*	whether it has changed recently? *It hasn't really changed, but there are more tourists and less people are living in Venice.*

2. Show this part of the DVD again if necessary and then ask the students to discuss the questions. The main aim of this exercise is to get the students thinking about and discussing what makes a good answer rather than to make a comparison of the candidates.

Answers

- Which questions do Inmi and Leonardo answer well? – *In fact, both Inmi and Leonardo answer all these questions well. They both give reasonably extended answers, particularly in question 3, where they do not just say whether their town/city has changed, but describe in what ways they have changed. Inmi is more hesitant than Leonardo, and gives the impression of being less comfortable speaking in English.*

- Which questions could they have answered better? – *They both give reasonably coherent and extended answers. Inmi loses some fluency in both questions 1 and 2 because of problems with and self-correction of is/are. Both Inmi and Leonardo could have picked up on the use of the present perfect in question 3 and used it in their response – Leonardo says that Venice doesn't change. It is a useful skill for students to listen to the tense cue in the question.*

- Who do you think gave the best answers in this part of the test and why? – *Students may disagree here, but in general Leonardo is more fluent, although Inmi is also willing to give extended answers. Both candidates have their strengths and weaknesses. Inmi is very clear, although her speech is a little mechanical in rhythm and would benefit from more chunking. Leonardo makes a fairly basic lexical error in 'changement' and is also a little hesitant at times.*

■ Optional activity: Game (10 minutes)

Although there are no irregular past tense forms in this exercise, you may like to have a quick practice of irregular past forms before moving on to **Task Four**, if students are likely to have a problem with these. You could do this through chain or group stories in which students are given verbs in the present and have to create a story in the past, selecting the correct irregular past forms.

Alternatively, you could practise them through a game such as 'Grammar Tennis': students are in groups of three, with two players and an umpire. The first player 'serves' a verb in the present or infinitive, the second responds with the past simple, and the first player 'returns' the past participle. The second player then 'plays' a new verb in the present or infinitive. This continues until the umpire declares there is a fault and awards the point to the winning student. A new verb is then 'served'.

■ Task Four: Language focus – tenses (5 minutes)

Part 1 aims to cover a range of tenses. Ask the students to complete the activity and then compare their answers in pairs before giving class feedback.

Answers (in bold)

1. I normally **live** in Seoul, but I **am living** in Cambridge at the moment.

2. Seoul **has changed** a lot recently. Ten years ago it **didn't have** convenient public transport.

3. I **haven't lived** here for long. I **moved** here three years ago.

4. Maybe my town **will change** in the future, I **don't really know**.

In question 2 you may like to point out that 'have' is a main verb here and, therefore, the past is formed with the auxiliary verb 'do'.

■ Task Five: Vocabulary brainstorm (2)   (5 minutes)

Another topic that may be covered at this stage is 'Work or Study'.

Ask the students to brainstorm useful vocabulary and phrases related to their work or study.

■ Task Six: Questions and answers (2)   (15 minutes)

Ask the students in pairs to think up four questions about this topic using a range of tenses. The fourth box allows them to provide a final question in any tense they wish.

Suggested answers

Now	What kind of work do you do? Do you like your work? Do you need any special skills for your work? What school or college are you at? What subjects are you studying? Do you like your job/school/college?
In the past	When did you start your work? Why did you choose this kind of work? Has your work changed much? Did you have to do any training for your work? What were your favourite subjects when you were younger? Why did you choose the subjects you are studying?
In the future	Do you think you will do different work in the future? Will you do this job for a long time? Will you do any more training for your job? Will you stay at this school/college for a long time? Will you continue to study these subjects in the future? Will your subjects be useful for your future work?
Your choice	In this section, students can add a question in any tense, so you would expect a wide range which might include any issues relating to work or study, such as what they like and dislike about it, what they would like to specialise in, skills needed, group work, etc.

Tell the students to find another partner and take it in turns to ask and answer questions.

This worksheet is based on Part 1 of the IELTS Speaking test. The whole of Part 1, including the introductions and the introductory topic covered in Worksheet 1, takes four to five minutes. The two topics covered in this worksheet, therefore, take about two to three minutes. These topics are designed to elicit information and opinions from the candidates about familiar subjects. As in the introductory topic, they cover a range of tenses and functions.

Time needed: 1 hour 10 minutes (1 hour 20 minutes with Optional Task)

■ Task One: Vocabulary brainstorm (5 minutes)

In pairs or groups, get the students to brainstorm vocabulary and phrases related to **Photos** and **Free time**. This will prepare them to carry out **Task Two**, in which they interview each other. You could follow this with a feedback session in which you build up mind maps of useful vocabulary and phrases on the board.

■ Task Two: Questions and answers (15 minutes)

1. Get the students to read the questions and carry out the interview in pairs. One student could ask the questions on photos and the other on free time. However, if more practice is needed, then each student can ask each set of questions. Many of the questions are followed by the word 'Why' in brackets. Point out to the students that the purpose of this is to enable the interlocutor to elicit further information if it has not been provided already, and that this should not deter candidates from giving a full answer to the initial question.

   Let's talk about photos now.

   - How often do you take photos? [Why/Why not?]

   - Do you prefer taking photos of people or of places? [Why?]

   - What do you do with the photos you take? [Why/Why not?]

   - Do you think the way people take photos is changing? [Why/Why not?]

   Let's talk about free time now.

   - How much free time do you normally have? [Why/Why not?]

   - What do you like doing best in your free time? [Why?]

   - Have your leisure activities changed much since you were young? [Why/Why not?]

   - If you had more free time, how would you spend it? [Why?]

2. Now show Inmi and Leonardo doing this part of the test on the DVD (Inmi: 01.53–04.41; Leonardo: 01.44–05.03). Ask the students to discuss with each other how effective their answers were in comparison with those of Inmi and Leonardo. They may also like to compare any differences in content between their answers.

■ Task Three: Watch and listen (20 minutes)

1. Show this part of the DVD again and ask the students to make notes in the table on what they hear. Ask them to compare their notes in pairs before going through the answers.

Answers

What does Inmi say about ...	What does Leonardo say about ...
How often she takes photos? *Every month.*	How often he takes photos? *When he goes on a trip and sees new places.*
Whether she prefers taking photos of people or places and why? *People – because of their different facial expressions.*	Whether he prefers taking photos of people or places and why? *People – because you can get pictures of places from websites or buy postcards.*
What she does with the photos she takes? *She writes down memories related to the photos.*	What he does with the photos he takes? *He puts them on his laptop and sometimes looks at them again to remind himself.*
Whether the way people take photos is changing? *People used to put their photos in an album and now they put them on a website.*	Whether the way people take photos is changing? *Digital cameras mean that people take many more pictures, often of unimportant things.*
How much free time she normally has? *2 or 3 hours a day.*	How much free time he normally has? *It depends. When he has exams he does not have much free time, but at other times he has either the morning or the afternoon free.*
What she likes doing best in her free time? *She likes keeping a diary.*	What he likes doing best in his free time? *He likes reading, watching movies or going out with friends.*
How she would spend more free time? *She would like to read more.*	Whether his leisure activities have changed much since he was young? *They haven't changed much. He just likes different books and movies.*

Ask the students to compare their notes with another student.

2. Play this part of the DVD again if necessary, and ask the students to discuss the questions. The main purpose of this task is to raise student awareness of the need to give extended and coherent responses, and to display a range of language rather than merely focusing on accuracy.

Suggested answers

- Which questions do Inmi and Leonardo answer well? – *Inmi answers the questions on photos well. She gives good extended responses both to how often she takes photos and also to why she prefers taking photos of people, using the opportunity to demonstrate some good lexis, e.g. 'facial expressions'. She also answers the question on what she likes doing in her free time well, giving a good response on why she likes keeping a diary.*

  Leonardo also answers the questions on photos well. He gives well-extended answers on the reason for his preference for photos of people and also on how the way people take photos is changing. His answers on free time are slightly less complete but are generally coherent and to the point. He takes the opportunity to display a range of structures, e.g. 'when I am going to do a trip ...', 'I used to ...'.

- Were there any questions they could have answered better? – *Inmi does not answer all the questions on free time as well as she might have. When asked how much free time she has she seems unsure about how to extend her answer and so repeats herself. In this case, she does not need to give a more extended answer. Inmi is also a little incoherent about reading English books. She seems to be unsure about the question on what she does with her photos, but comes up with an interesting answer. She often hesitates to collect her thoughts before answering, and this would sound more natural if she used a filler such as 'well ...', 'actually ...' or 'in fact ...'. In the final question, when asked what she would do if she had more free time, Inmi neglects to take up the cue of the conditional and answers 'I want ...' instead.*

Leonardo, in general, answers all the questions well, although he uses a conditional 'I'd like' when asked what he likes doing in his free time, and does not seem able to think of any real ways in which his free time activities have changed.

- Who do you think gave the best answers in this part of the test? – *Students may well have different views on this because their performances vary. However, in general, despite some inaccuracies such as 'unuseful, watch (see) new places', Leonardo shows a greater lexical and grammatical range, and is more fluent and ready to respond than Inmi.*

■ Task Four: Focus on language   (15 minutes)

1. Expressions of liking and disliking

   Both Inmi and Leonardo say that they prefer taking pictures of people. Describing likes and dislikes is a common feature of Part 1. Ask students to look at the following expressions of liking and disliking and decide whether they are followed by the infinitive (with or without 'to') or the gerund ('-ing'). They may notice the general pattern that verbs of liking are followed by '-ing' when talking about likes in general, and by the infinitive when talking about a more specific situation ('I like to swim before I have my lunch') or wants ('I would like to swim with dolphins').

   Answers (in bold)

Like + **-ing or to (although -ing is more common when talking about likes in general)**	Would like + **to**
Enjoy + **-ing**	Love + **-ing**
Prefer + **-ing**	Would rather + **infinitive without to**
Hate + **-ing**	Can't stand + **-ing**

   Ask the students to practise these verbal constructions in pairs by discussing things that they like and dislike using these verbs. You may like to give them some ideas of topics, e.g. on holiday, in the evening, with your friends, foods, music.

2. Adverbs of frequency

   The first question on photos asks **how often** the candidate takes photos, and the first question on free time asks how much free time the candidate **normally** has. In the question on taking photos, Leonardo says 'I **usually** take photos when I go on a trip.'

   Ask the students to put the following adverbs of frequency in order starting with the most frequent and ending with the least frequent. Note that some of these adverbs have the same meaning.

sometimes	occasionally	seldom	from time to time	always	rarely	often	frequently
never	usually						

   Answers

always	usually	frequently	sometimes	from time to time	rarely	never
		often		occasionally	seldom	

   Ask the students to discuss in pairs what they do at the weekend using these adverbs.

■ Task Five: Talking about a topic   (15 minutes)

The topics below are only suggestions. You could choose any other familiar topics. Ask the students in pairs to write four questions on one of the topics. You could either allocate a topic to each pair or let them choose their own. It might be useful to remind them that each topic is designed to elicit a range of tenses and functions, so that they consider this when creating their questions. Students should then find another partner and take it in turns to ask and answer their questions.

| music | sport | travel | holidays | reading | films | TV | clothes | spare time |
| shopping | transport | | | | | | | |

■ Optional Task: 20 questions   (10 minutes)

Put the students in groups of two to six. Ask them to think of a free time activity, without telling the rest of their group. The group then have 20 questions to guess their activity. They should only give short responses with 'Yes' or 'No', e.g. 'Yes, I do', 'No, I haven't'.

Traditionally in this game, the response is only 'Yes' or 'No'. However, in this case, it is intended to give further practice in short responses.

IELTS Speaking test
Teacher's Notes

This worksheet is based on Part 2 of the IELTS Speaking test. The aim of this worksheet is to raise student awareness of the requirements and timing of the task, and to give them practice in using the preparation time profitably, and in organising and producing a two-minute individual speaking turn.

Photocopy Task Card 1 provided at the beginning of this book or, before the lesson, print it out from the DVD, and make sure you have enough copies to give one to each student.

Time needed: 1 hour

■ Task One: Fill the gaps   (5 minutes)

Ask the students to read the introduction to Part 2 of the test and complete the gaps with the missing words from the box.

Check their answers.

Answers (in bold)

Now, I'm going to give you a **topic** and I'd like you to talk about it for one to **two** minutes. Before you **talk**, you'll have one minute to **think** about what you're going to **say**. You can make some **notes** if you wish. Do you understand?

Here's some **paper** and a pencil for **making** notes and here's your topic. I'd like you to **describe** a situation when someone that you didn't know helped you.

■ Task Two: Making notes   (5 minutes)

1. Give a copy of Task Card 1 to each student and allow them one minute to write brief notes on what they are going to say on this topic. Remind them that they are not writing an essay or connected prose. The aim is to build up ideas and useful language for the task.

2. Ask the students to compare their notes with a partner.

   Discuss with the students useful strategies for preparing the topic, e.g. mind mapping. These will be covered in more detail in Worksheet 4.

■ Task Three: Watch and listen   (20 minutes)

1. Play the section on the DVD of Inmi doing this part of the test (00.00–03.11) and ask the students to complete the table on their worksheets. Then ask them the three questions below the table.

Answers

What the situation was	She had been at a farewell party for a friend who was leaving, and she got lost on the way home.
When and where it happened	When: 1 month ago and after 2.00 a.m. Where: In a town – looking for Histon Road (in fact, it was in Cambridge but she doesn't say this).
How the person helped her	The person took her to her house.
How she felt in that situation	She felt very scared when she was lost.

- How easy does Inmi find it to do this part of the test? – *Inmi actually seems to enjoy this part of the test. She has no problem thinking of a situation, and finds it easy to fill the two minutes by giving the background to the main situation – this is a very good way of dealing with this sort of task. She is hesitant at times, but more because of her lack of fluency and confidence in speaking in English rather than because of any problems with the task itself.*

- Do you think that her notes helped her to do the task? – *She doesn't seem to use her notes, but they probably helped her to organise her thoughts beforehand. In fact, it is quite hard to work out what she wrote in her notes, although they probably contained a brief summary of what happened. At times she finds it difficult to access the language she needs to complete the task, and she occasionally becomes hesitant while searching for the necessary words and structures. It might, therefore, have helped her to jot down some key lexis on her notes.*

- Did she use the prompts on the card to help her organise the task? – *She did seem to use them, because she covered all the prompts very clearly. It is possible that the prompts helped her to organise her task, but in fact a narrative is inherently easier to organise than a more descriptive task. It would be helpful here to point out to the students that the prompts not only provide ideas but can often provide a helpful way of organising their talk.*

2. Play the section of the DVD (00.00–02.58) on Leonardo doing this part of the test and ask the students to complete the table on their worksheets. Then ask them the three questions below the table.

Answers

What the situation was	He was playing on a beach and got lost. He found a couple of children who helped him.
When and where it happened	When: He was a child, about 5 years old. At 7.00 in the evening. Where: On holiday – on a beach in Sardinia.
How the person helped him	Two children helped him. They asked him what the matter was, took his hand and walked along the beach with him until he found his parents.
How he felt in that situation	He doesn't really say – probably because the two minutes were up before he finished his story. He does say that it was difficult because it was a long beach and it all looked the same.

- How easy does Leonardo find it to do this part of the test? – *Leonardo seems to find it relatively easy to do this part of the test. His contribution is fairly fluent, accurate and well organised, and he provides plenty of detail. He has no problems speaking for the full two minutes and clearly could have continued for longer if necessary. He has effective control of narrative tenses, using the past continuous for the background and setting the scene, and past simple for the main events. He has some problems with reported speech. (Note that **Task Five** provides some practice exercises on reported speech.)*

- Do you think his notes helped him to do the task? – *There is no sign of him actually referring to his notes, but we can probably assume that, as with Inmi, he uses his notes to help him gather his thoughts before talking. He could have done this a little more effectively if he had decided during the minute whether he was helped by boys, girls or a boy and a girl, since the hesitation over this does slightly reduce the effectiveness of his talk, and it is not important whether they were boys or girls.*

- How does he organise the task? – *Leonardo organises his task both by using the points on the Task Card, and by using a traditional narrative organisation of setting the scene before giving the main facts. He tells us in plenty of detail about the time and place of the incident, before moving on to what actually happened. This is effective, and involves the listener in the narrative. We can assume that if he had talked for longer then he would have explained how he felt, but the effectiveness of his talk is in no way reduced by not having time for this.*

3. Ask the students to look again at their notes and consider how helpful they will be for their talk. Ask them to add one or two ideas to extend their talk if they need to speak for longer. You may consider it worthwhile to take a minute for them to redo their notes in the light of their prior discussion of the notes and Inmi and Leonardo's performance on the DVD.

■ Task Four: Focus on pronunciation   (10 minutes)

When speaking, students often focus on phonemes at the expense of prosodic features such as rhythm, stress and intonation. Students from syllable-timed languages often find it difficult to reproduce the rhythm and stress of a stress-timed language such as English. It might, therefore, be helpful to use the following phrases related to the topic to practise these features. You could also point out that when candidates become hesitant, as Inmi did at times, they tend to focus on the production of individual words at the expense of effective chunking.

The sentences on the worksheet have all been taken from Inmi's presentation, and show some good uses of language and complex structures such as:

- infinitive of purpose in sentence 1 – to go back home

- prepositional phrase in sentence 2 – after getting off the bus

- comparative clauses in sentence 3 – the more ... the more ...

- in sentence 4, she actually says 'When I was walking along the street, I met a man, **he** was going to work. You might like to point out that this has been changed in this exercise into the more effective use of a relative clause as a way of linking ideas.

Ask the students to work with a partner to practise reading the sentences related to the topic. Focus on:

- stressing the key words and ideas

- linking words in phrases together

- chunking the words into meaningful groups.

The answers below show the main stressed words and chunks, although it is important to note that some chunks are more closely linked than others, e.g. 'I took a bus with my friend' is more closely linked than 'To go back home I took a bus'. Equally, some stressed words will have greater stress than others, e.g. the strong stress on 'the **more** ...' in order to convey meaning and emphasise the extent of her difficulty. Other points that may be worth pointing out are: the stress of the adverbial particle in phrasal verbs, particularly when not followed by a noun ('where I **got off**'); and the weak pronunciation of auxiliary verbs (in sentence 4, 'walking' is stressed but not 'was'). A helpful guideline for students is that, in general, it is nouns and main verbs that are stressed, adjectives usually receiving a weaker stress, and such elements as pronouns, auxiliaries, articles and prepositions being very weak and often using a schwa. This general guideline can be varied in order to convey specific meaning and to stress what the speaker sees as key elements of what is being said.

Answers (stressed words in bold)

1. To **go** back **home**/I **took** a **bus/**with my **friend**.

2. I **knew** where I **got off**,/ but after **getting off** the **bus/** I got **lost**. ('Got' is a verb that is fairly empty of meaning, so it is 'lost' that conveys the main message here.)

3. The **more** I **walked** along the **street**/ the more **difficult** it was for me/ to **find** my **way home**. (The second 'more' is not stressed because it is 'difficult' which contains the new, and therefore important, information here.)

4. When I was **walking** along the **street**,/ I **met** a **man** who was **going** to **work**.

■ Task Five: Focus on language   (10 minutes)

Both Inmi and Leonardo attempt to use reported speech in their talks, but with limited success.

Ask the students to put the direct speech structures into reported speech. They are either taken from or relate to Leonardo's presentation. The sentences include indirect/reported statements, questions and imperatives, so could be quite difficult. These can either be used as a quick revision exercise or, if you feel that they will be difficult for your students, you can revise this topic and find some supplementary exercises to do first.

Answers

1. 'I am lost.' – (Example) *He said (that) he was lost.*

2. 'How old are you?' – *They asked him how old he was.*

   N.B. Students often find it difficult to remember that indirect questions are no longer questions, and that they should therefore use the word order of statements rather than questions.

3. 'What are you doing here?' – *They asked him what he was doing there.*

4. 'Don't worry. Come with us and we will show you.' – *They told him not to worry, to come with them, and (that) they would show him.*

   N.B. This sentence is quite difficult because it starts with two reported imperatives, one negative and one positive, and then ends with a reported statement.

■ Task Six: Talk time   (10 minutes)

1. Ask the students to give a two-minute talk to a partner based on their notes and their discussion of the DVD. They will also need a copy of Task Card 1 in front of them as they carry out their talk.

2. Ask the students to then listen to their partner's talk and time it for two minutes.

3. Ask the students to discuss the following questions with their partner:

   • How easy did you find the talk?

   • Did you find your notes helpful? Why/Why not?

   • How did you organise your task?

   • How could you extend your task if needed?

This worksheet is designed to give further practice in Part 2 of the IELTS Speaking test. It is useful for students to practise this part of the test as much as possible, in order for them to gain confidence in talking for an extended time. It is also important for them to work out how to use their one-minute preparation time effectively.

Photocopy Task Card 2 provided at the beginning of this book and Task Card 3 provided at the end of this book or, before the lesson, print them out from the DVD, and make sure you have enough copies to give each Task Card to each student.

Time needed: 55 minutes

■ Task One: Language focus – cohesive devices   (5 minutes)

These are an important aid for students in structuring their talk. Ask the students in pairs to work out which of these cohesive devices have similar meanings. This should be a fairly brief and simple task. The main aim is to raise student awareness of cohesive devices and to encourage them to practise these devices later on when they do their presentations.

Answers

At first	After that	In the end
In the beginning	Later on	Eventually

■ Task Two: Making notes   (5 minutes)

This task is designed to increase students' awareness of how to make the most of their one-minute preparation time. Candidates sometimes have a tendency to write mini-essays in their preparation time, and this can be difficult to refer to while speaking. Mind maps are a helpful way to encourage the recording and organisation of ideas and lexis. Give a copy of Task Card 2 to each student and allow them exactly one minute for making notes. Then ask them to compare and talk about their mind map and notes with a partner.

■ Task Three: Talk time   (10 minutes)

1. Students should then carry out the two-minute talk in turns with their partner, using the task card and their notes. This talk will probably include a sequence of events, so encourage the students to try to incorporate some of the cohesive devices related to sequencing events within their talk.

    While one student is talking, the other should be taking notes to check that their partner covers all the points in the task. They may also like to note down the cohesive devices used and any other useful words or phrases. If you have the facilities, the students might like to record the talk to listen to later or, otherwise, you could suggest that they do this for further practice at home.

2. After the talk, students should discuss with their partner how the task was completed and how useful the mind map notes were. Encourage them to discuss whether there are any other ways of making notes that they would find more effective. They will then have a chance to try these out in the second practice task below.

■ Task Four: Language focus – cohesive devices (2)   (5 minutes)

This task builds upon the awareness of cohesive devices encouraged in **Task One**. Ask the students to do this exercise in pairs, allocating two cohesive devices to each function.

Answers

Giving the first opinion or fact	To begin with, First of all
Comparing or contrasting	Whereas, On the other hand
Introducing a statement or opinion	Actually, Basically
Giving an example or more specific information	Particularly, Specifically

■ Task Five: Making notes (2)   (5 minutes)

This task will give the students further practice, and a chance to put into practice anything that they have learned from **Task Two** in this worksheet. It will also give them a chance to practise the cohesive devices from **Task Four**.

Give a copy of Task Card 3 to each student and allow them one minute exactly to make notes about this topic in the box provided. They can either repeat the mind map technique or they can try out any other technique that they think they will find more helpful, e.g. listing or making notes in their L1.

■ Task Six: Talk time (2)   (10 minutes)

1. The students should carry out the two-minute talk in turns with their partner using the task card and their notes. In their talk they should try to incorporate some of the cohesive devices from **Task Four**.

    While one student is speaking, the other should be taking notes to check that they cover all the points in the task. As in **Task Three**, they could also note down cohesive devices and any other useful lexis used.

2. Ask the students to discuss with their partner how the task was completed and how useful their notes were.

■ Task Seven: Game – Just a Minute   (15 minutes)

For this game you will need a die and some way of timing a minute per group. A minute timer or stopwatch is ideal but any watch with a minute indicator would do. If you do not have a die, you could put the topics on folded pieces of paper and each student could pick a topic.

The students should be in groups of four or five. One student could be referee and decide whether the challenges are to be allowed, or the group could vote on challenges.

One student should throw a die and look at the topic with the same number. This student then has to talk for one minute on the topic without hesitating or deviating from the subject. Any other student in the group can challenge if the speaker hesitates or deviates from the subject. A successful challenger then takes over the topic for the rest of the minute. This challenger can in turn be challenged by any other member of the group. A point is scored for each successful completion of a minute. The next student in the group then throws the die until a different number comes up and begins to speak about the topic with the corresponding number. The game continues until all the topics have been covered or all the students have had the chance to speak.

You may like to point out to the students the useful nature of fillers such as: in general, actually, well, of course, some people think that, in my opinion, as far as I know, this is an interesting question. If there is enough time, a second round of Just a Minute could be played in which students gain points by using an appropriate filler.

1. Music   2. Sport   3. Travel   4. Holidays   5. Reading   6. Films

Possible further topics are: TV, Clothes, Spare time, Shopping, Transport, Friends, Celebrations, Weather, A family member, Famous people, The internet.

IELTS Speaking test
Teacher's Notes

This worksheet is based on Part 3 of the IELTS Speaking test. This part of the test lasts 4–5 minutes and is designed to take the discussion related to the topic covered in Part 2 into more general areas. In this part, candidates no longer talk about themselves and their experiences, but about people, beliefs and experiences in general. The questions are designed to elicit a range of functions such as describing, comparing, suggesting, agreeing or disagreeing.

Time needed: 1 hour

■ Task One: Fill the gaps   (5 minutes)

Ask the students to watch Leonardo's examiner introduce this part of the test on the DVD (00.00–00.15) and fill in the missing words.

Answers (in bold)

We've been **talking** about a situation **when** someone you didn't **know** helped you, and I'd like **to discuss** (2 words) with you one or two more **general** questions related to this. Let's consider **first** of all children **helping** others.

■ Task Two: Vocabulary brainstorm   (5 minutes)

Ask the students to brainstorm words and phrases related to children helping other people. This could be done in pairs or groups and could take the form of a mind map. You might like to suggest some general areas such as helping in the home, or helping in the community.

■ Task Three: Questions and answers   (10 minutes)

Ask the students to read the questions and practise asking and answering them in pairs.

- What kinds of thing can children do to help in the home?

- How can children best learn to be helpful to others?

- In what ways can schools encourage children to help the community?

■ Task Four: Watch and listen   (20 minutes)

1. Ask the students to watch Inmi doing this part of the test (00.00–03.05) and to complete the chart as they listen. They can do this first individually and then compare their answers in pairs.

Things children can do to help in the home	They can organise (tidy) their rooms. They can use the vacuum cleaner.
How children can learn to be helpful to others	Mainly through seeing their parents being helpful. They can also learn by being told about it both by their parents and teachers.
Ways schools can encourage children to help the community	Show them videos and encourage them to help orphans.

2. Ask the students to discuss the questions with a partner.

Suggested answers

- What do you think Inmi does well? – *She gives well-extended and thoughtful answers and is able to express her ideas reasonably well despite limitations and errors in vocabulary.*

- What do you think she could do better? – *Inmi seems to find this part more difficult than Part 2. She hesitates quite a lot and speaks quite slowly. This is sometimes while she is searching for ideas but is often while she searches for words or grammar. She also finds it hard to think of ideas of how schools can encourage children to help the community and becomes rather repetitive on the idea of orphans (which she mispronounces). She starts most of her replies with an 'ah ...' and a silence. It would help her to use some phrase to help her buy time such as: 'well ...', 'that's an interesting question ...'.*

- Do you agree with her ideas on children helping others? – *Students will, of course, come up with different responses, but encourage them to justify their responses.*

3. Ask the students to watch Leonardo doing this part of the test (00.00–02.24) and complete the chart. They can do this first individually and then compare their answers in pairs.

Answers

Things children can do to help in the home	First by being tidy. Later by laying the table or tidying their rooms.
How children can learn to be helpful to others	Having their parents as a model. Education by their parents.
Ways schools can encourage children to help the community	Show different ways to help. Tell them about associations they can join. Explain how they can help.

4. Ask the students to discuss the questions on the worksheet with a partner.

Suggested answers

- What do you think Leonardo does well? – *He gives well-extended and full answers to the questions and he is able to paraphrase fairly successfully (prepare the table). He has some good lexis – 'tidy the room', 'a good model'.*

- What do you think he could do better? – *At times his answers become a little incoherent, e.g. when he is trying to explain how schools can encourage children to help in the community. As with Inmi, he also could use 'well ...' to buy time as he thinks about his responses rather than saying 'er', or he could use a phrase such as 'I'm not sure but ...', 'I've never really thought about that but. ...'.*

  He also tends to die away at the end of some responses when he can't think of anything further to say – it might help him to think of some final comment such as 'actually, I'm not really sure what's best'.

- Do you agree with his ideas on children helping others? – *Students will, of course, come up with different responses, but encourage them to justify their responses.*

▪ Task Five: Focus on language   (20 minutes)

These are useful aspects of language arising from or related to this part of the interview. Point out to the students that the phrases taken from the interviews were not necessarily wrong.

1. They could do this activity in pairs, or individually and then check in pairs.

   Answers (in bold)

   - Young **children** often enjoy **helping** round the house.

   - **It depends** on the age of the children.

   - They can learn **to be** helpful through **watching** others.

   - They might be **interested in helping** orphans.

   - The teacher knows **how** to teach **them** to help others.

   - The first thing is being tidy and **not throwing** their things on the floor.

   - They must **do** something **to help** their parents.

   - The first model **is** their parents.

   - Show the different things **which** they can do to help.

   - That's **rather** a difficult question.

2. Ask the students to match a word from column A with a word or phrase in column B to describe some household tasks. They could do this either in pairs, or individually and then check in pairs.

   Note that some verbs, e.g. *tidy up*, can take various options.

   Answers

A	B
make	the beds
lay	the table
iron	the clothes
do	the washing up
tidy up	the toys
vacuum	the carpet
put out	the rubbish
cut	the grass
look after	the younger children

   They could then suggest any other household tasks they can think of.

   If you wanted to lead into further lexical development, you could point out the use of the particle 'up' in the phrasal verb 'tidy up' and look at other examples of how this can add the idea of 'completion' or 'fastening' (clean up, brush up, cut up, do up, tie up, wrap up, etc.).

IELTS Speaking test
Teacher's Notes

This worksheet is based on Part 3 of the IELTS Speaking test. It deals with the second set of questions and gives further practice in asking and answering questions for this part of the test.

Time needed: 1 hour

■ Task One: Questions and answers   (10 minutes)

Ask the students to read the questions on working for other people without payment and practise asking and answering them in pairs. Either one student can ask all the questions and then the other student can, or they each ask and answer one at a time.

- What types of voluntary work are most popular in your country?

- How do you think individuals might benefit from doing voluntary work?

- In which ways can voluntary work improve life for the community?

■ Task Two: Watch and listen   (20 minutes)

1. Show Inmi doing this part of the test on the DVD (03.06–04.45) and ask the students to complete the chart on their worksheet.

   Answers

Popular types of voluntary work in her country	There is a lot: teaching children and preparing meals.
How individuals might benefit from doing voluntary work	They can feel very fulfilled.
How voluntary work can improve life for the community	It encourages people to have relationships and interaction.

2. Ask the students to discuss the questions with a partner.

   Suggested answers

   - What do you think Inmi does well? – *She is still trying to give extended answers, but definitely finds this more difficult as the test progresses. Although she has some problems with finding the appropriate words, she still comes up with some good lexis (relationships, interaction).*

   - What do you think she could do better? – *Despite her attempts to give extended answers, she treats this more like a question and answer session than a discussion. In other words she tries to think of 'an answer' rather than exploring the topic. She could perhaps have done this in question 1 by comparing what people of different ages might do, and in question 2 by exploring different reasons for people doing (or not doing) voluntary work. If voluntary work is not very common in a particular country, this could also be an interesting topic to explore. Despite her occasional good lexis, Inmi is hesitant as she searches for lexis in this part of the test and sometimes uses inappropriate words such as fulfilment (fulfilled).*

   - Were her answers on working for other people without payment the same as yours? – *Students will have different responses here, but encourage them to discuss and justify their answers, and to extend them if necessary to develop a discussion.*

3. Show Leonardo doing this part of the test on the DVD (02.25–05.04) and ask the students to complete the chart on their worksheet.

Answers

Popular types of voluntary work in his country	Helping old people. Helping people in jail/prisoners – teaching them while they are in prison, and helping them to integrate back into society when they come out.
The age of people who normally do voluntary work	Generally it is retired people, because they have more free time.
How individuals might benefit from doing voluntary work	They get good feedback – it makes them feel useful and important.
How voluntary work can improve life for the community	It provides help for the poorest and the old and offers services that the government doesn't. It makes the community a better place to live in.

4. Ask the students to discuss the questions with a partner.

Suggested answers

- What do you think Leonardo does well? – *Leonardo generally manages this part of the test very well. His answers are thoughtful and extended and he manages to express himself very well without too much hesitation. He keeps up the flow of the discussion by buying time with phrases such as 'Actually, I don't know exactly ...' and also uses the repetition of the question to gain thinking time, e.g. 'I think individuals can benefit ...'.*

- What do you think he could do better? – *He really carries out the task very well. However, he does occasionally hesitate to search for words and displays a few language problems in verb phrases such as 'teach to the people' 'stop to work', and in using 'another people' rather than 'other people'.*

- Were his answers on working for other people without payment the same as yours? – *Students will have different responses here, but encourage them to discuss and justify their answers, and to extend them if necessary to develop a discussion.*

■ Task Three: Focus on language   (15 minutes)

These are short exercises designed to check two areas of language, which are often useful in the test. Alternatively, you may find that your students have their own specific mistakes and weaknesses, and you might prefer to spend more time on these.

Students should do these exercises individually and then compare them with another student before whole class feedback.

1. Leonardo talks about making the community a better place to live in. In each part of the test it is helpful to be able to make comparisons.

   Tell students to complete the sentences on their worksheet with an appropriate comparative phrase.

   Answers (in bold)

   - Young people do not do voluntary work **as much** as retired people.

   - Young people do voluntary work **less** than retired people.

   - Older people do voluntary work **more frequently than** young people.

   - Wealthy people do not need nearly **as much help as** poor people.

   - Some communities are **better than** others.

2. Inmi tries to say that voluntary work can be very *fulfilling*. Adjectives of emotions and feelings usually have two forms, e.g. relaxing, relaxed. Ask students to complete the sentences on the worksheet using the correct form of the adjective.

Answers (in bold)

- Helping others can be very **fulfilling**.

- You can feel very **fulfilled** when helping others.

- I was **amazed** by how much they did to help.

- It is **amazing** how much they managed to help.

- Some voluntary work can be really **interesting**.

- Retired people might be most **interested** in voluntary work.

■ Task Four: Game – Making Comparisons   (15 minutes)

Look back at the list of tasks for helping in the house in Worksheet 5, **Task Five**, Activity 2. Ask the students in pairs to choose two of these tasks and then write five sentences making comparisons between them.

They should label the tasks as 'x' and 'y' and then read them out to the rest of the class who must guess which two tasks they are comparing.

You may like to provide or elicit some useful ways of making comparisons first. One good way is to do an example comparison as a whole class first. On the board write:

Making the bed

Cutting the grass

Ask the students to suggest serious or funny comparisons, e.g. 'Making the bed is easier to do in your nightclothes than cutting the grass.' Encourage them to use a wide range of comparison phrases and if necessary write some on the board to encourage their use. A possible list is as follows:

-er/est

more/most

less/the least

as … as

adverbs to highlight or downplay – much bigger, slightly bigger, not nearly as … as, not quite as … as

by far the most …

while

whereas

on the other hand

This worksheet is based on the whole of the IELTS Speaking test. It provides a full test, which is intended as a final practice for students to put together all that they have learnt in the earlier worksheets.

Photocopy Task Card 4 provided at the end of this book or, before the lesson, print it out from the DVD, and make sure you have enough copies to give one to each student.

Time needed: (45–60 minutes)

■ Task One: You are the examiner!   (45–60 minutes)

1. Put the students in pairs. Each pair should have access to a watch or clock, so that they can keep each part of the test to the required timing. If this is not possible, the teacher could indicate when to start and stop each part.

    First, student A should be the 'examiner' and student B the 'candidate'. The 'examiner' should look at the worksheet containing what they should say in each part of the test. You will also need to copy or print Task Card 4 to give to the 'examiner' along with a blank sheet of paper and a pencil. The 'examiner' will need to hand these to the 'candidate' at the appropriate time in Part 2. It would also be useful for the 'examiner' to have an extra copy of the Task Card to refer to while the 'candidate' is speaking and check that they covered all the points in the task.

2. During the test the 'examiner' could make notes on the worksheet and, at the end of the test, could give brief feedback to the 'candidate'. The students should then swap roles and do the test again with the other student as 'examiner', who can also make notes and give brief feedback at the end.

    While the students are doing the test, go round the pairs and note down any points for whole-class feedback or language development at the end of the test. If you feel you have any students who would like to perform the test, or part of the test, in front of the whole class, then you could finish the activity with this.

PART 1 (4–5 minutes)

Let's talk about what you do. Do you work or are you a student?

If the candidate works:

- What kind of work do you do?

- Why did you choose this kind of work?

- Do you prefer working in a team or working alone? [Why/Why not?]

If the candidate studies:

- What subject do you study?

- Why did you choose this subject?

- Do you prefer studying in a group or studying alone? [Why/Why not?]

Now let's talk about sports.

- What is your favourite sport? [Why?]

- How often do you play sports yourself? [Why/Why not?]

- Do you prefer watching sports live or on TV? [Why/Why not?]

- If you had the chance to meet a famous sports person, who would you choose? [Why/Why not?]

PART 2 (3–4 minutes)

Examiner: Now, I'm going to give you a topic and I'd like you to talk about it for one to two minutes. Before you talk, you'll have one minute to think about what you're going to say. You can make some notes if you wish. Do you understand?

Here's some paper and a pencil for making notes (*hand over blank paper and a pencil*) and here's your topic (*hand over topic*).

I'd like you to describe something that you would like to do in the future if you had the chance.

(*At the end of 1 minute's preparation:*)

All right? Can you start speaking now, please?

(*At the end of the 2 minutes, ask the following rounding-off question:*)

Do you like making plans for the future?

Thank you.

PART 3 (4–5 minutes)

Examiner: We've been talking about something that you would like to do in the future if you had the chance, and I'd like to discuss with you one or two more general questions related to this. Let's consider first of all ...

(Select one or two of the following sets of questions to develop a discussion:)

- Making plans for the future

  - What kinds of thing do people make plans for in their daily life?

  - Can you think of any reasons why some individuals are better than others at planning?

  - Do you think that important events are always more successful if they have been carefully planned?

- Predicting the future

  - What kinds of thing might people predict about the future?

  - What kinds of situation do businesses need to predict?

  - Do you think there might be any problems in predicting future events?

Examiner: Thank you very much. That is the end of the Speaking test.

This worksheet summarises the IELTS Speaking test and reviews the format and tasks.

Students should be able to complete this worksheet after watching the DVD and completing worksheets 1 to 7.

Time needed: 1 hour 5 minutes

■ Task One: Fill the gaps   (10 minutes)

Ask students to fill in the missing information about the Speaking test.

Answers (in bold)

1. The Speaking test lasts for **11–14** minutes.

2. There are **3** parts to the Speaking test.

3. The format is **1** candidate/s and **1** examiner/s.

4. In Part **1**, the examiner asks you about familiar personal topics.

5. In Part 2, the candidate speaks about a topic for **2** minutes.

6. In Part **3**, the discussion is more general.

■ Task Two: True or false?   (30 minutes)

Ask the students to read the statements and write 'True' or 'False' next to each one.

Answers

1. At the start of the test, the examiner will want to see your passport or identity card. – *True.*

2. The first set of questions in the test is always about your work or studies. – *False – it can be about where you live.*

3. The examiner will enter into a discussion with you in Part 1. – *False – the examiner asks specific questions in Part 1.*

4. In Part 2, you can choose the topic you speak about. – *False – the examiner will give you the topic.*

5. In Part 2, you have 2 minutes to prepare before you begin speaking. – *False – you have 1 minute.*

6. You can make notes in preparation for your talk in Part 2. – *True.*

7. In Part 2, after you have finished speaking, the examiner asks you 3 further questions. – *False – there is usually just one question, but occasionally two.*

8. Part 3 is about a different topic from the one in Part 2. – *False – it is connected to the topic in Part 2.*

9. In Part 3, the questions are general and not personal. – *True.*

After the students have checked their answers with a partner, show them the whole Speaking test on the DVD to see if they were right.

■ Task Three: Marking and assessment   (10 minutes)

Ask the students to put the pieces of advice for getting good marks in the correct box.

Answers

Assessment criteria	Advice
Fluency and Coherence	Try to develop your ideas logically and fluently. Try to connect your ideas together clearly. Try not to hesitate for too long before you speak.
Lexical Resource	Try to use interesting words and phrases, not just the same ones all the time. Try to be precise in the words you use.
Grammatical Range and Accuracy	Use a range of structures. Listen carefully to what you are saying, and correct any mistakes that you hear yourself make.
Pronunciation	Use intonation and stress to help convey meaning. Speak clearly and intelligibly.

■ Task Four: Preparation   (15 minutes)

This task is designed to encourage the students to consider how well prepared they are for the exam, and to plan what practice they need to do.

Ask the students to look at the areas in the table and put a mark from 1–3:

1	I am very confident	2	I need to practise	3	I need to do a lot more work to prepare

	My mark	*What I can do to improve*
Answering questions about familiar and personal topics in Part 1		
Talking for 2 minutes in Part 2		
Taking part in the general discussion in Part 3		

When students have completed the mark column of the chart, they should discuss with their partner what they can do to improve, and make notes in the table.

IELTS Speaking test
Student Worksheets

This section contains the nine Student Worksheets for IELTS:
- Introductory Worksheet – provides an introduction to the IELTS Speaking test as a whole
- Worksheet 1 – based on Part 1 of the Speaking test
- Worksheet 2 – based on Part 1 of the Speaking test
- Worksheet 3 – based on Part 2 of the Speaking test
- Worksheet 4 – based on Part 2 of the Speaking test
- Worksheet 5 – based on Part 3 of the Speaking test
- Worksheet 6 – based on Part 3 of the Speaking test
- Worksheet 7 – based on the whole of the Speaking test
- Worksheet 8 – provides a summary of the IELTS Speaking test and reviews its format and tasks.

The Student Worksheet pages of this book are photocopiable and you can also print copies from the Student Worksheets file on the DVD. For your class you will also need:
- the DVD
- for Part 2, the candidate task cards. You will find these inside the front and back covers of this book. There is also a file of this material on the DVD.

UNIVERSITY *of* CAMBRIDGE
ESOL Examinations

IELTS Speaking test
Student Worksheets

INTRODUCTORY
WORKSHEET

■ Aims of the DVD and worksheets

- to raise your awareness of the IELTS Speaking test
- to focus your attention on techniques that will improve your performance
- to provide opportunities for you to practise the language used in the different parts of the test.

Please note:

The DVD and worksheets are not intended as a forum for discussing grades. Although in certain questions we are asking you to look at the candidates' performance, it is with a view to improving your own performance and not for you to grade the candidates on the DVD.

The IELTS Speaking test on the DVD has been produced for teaching purposes only and is not a live exam. There are, therefore, no grades available.

■ Task One: General Information about the IELTS Speaking test

This worksheet focuses on general information about the IELTS Speaking test.

Fill in the missing information:

1. The length of the test is _____ minutes.

2. The normal format is _____ candidate/s and _____ examiner/s.

3. There are _____ parts to the test.

4. The Speaking test is worth _____ % of the whole IELTS test.

■ Task Two : Match the two

Look at the following information about each part of the Speaking test. Working in pairs, complete each statement in column A with one from column B.

Answers

A	B
Part 1 lasts for	gives the candidates a topic to speak about and asks a rounding-off question
In Part 1, the examiner	4–5 minutes
In Part 1, the candidate	gives general views and opinions on the topic
Part 2 lasts for	gives personal information
In Part 2, the examiner	4–5 minutes
In Part 2, the candidate	greets the candidate and asks questions selected from familiar topics
Part 3 lasts for	leads a general discussion of a more abstract nature connected to the Part 2 topic
In Part 3, the examiner	speaks for 1–2 minutes on a topic related to their experience
In Part 3, the candidate	3–4 minutes

This worksheet is based on the introductory section of Part 1 of the IELTS Speaking test.

■ Task One: Vocabulary brainstorm

Brainstorm useful vocabulary and phrases related to your home town or city.

■ Task Two: Questions and answers

1. Read the questions below. Work with a partner and ask and answer them in turn.

   • What do you like most about your home town/city? [Why?]

   • Is your home town/city a popular place for tourists to visit? [Why/Why not?]

   • Has your home town/city changed much in recent years? [How?]

 2. Now watch Inmi and Leonardo do the introductory section on the DVD. Were your answers longer or shorter than theirs?

■ Task Three: Watch and listen

 1. Watch this part of the DVD again and make notes in the table below.

What does Inmi say about ...	What does Leonardo say about ...
what she likes most about Seoul?	what he likes most about Venice?
Seoul's popularity with tourists?	Venice's popularity with tourists?
whether it has changed recently?	whether it has changed recently?

Compare your notes with other students in the group.

 2. Watch this part of the DVD again if necessary and then discuss these questions:

   • Which questions do Inmi and Leonardo answer well?

   • Which questions could they have answered better?

   • Who do you think gave the best answers in this part of the test and why?

■ Task Four: Language focus – tenses

Part 1 of the Speaking test aims to cover a range of tenses. Complete the following sentences with the correct tense of the words in brackets.

1. I normally _____ (live) in Seoul, but I _____ (live) in

   Cambridge at the moment.

2. Seoul _____ (change) a lot recently. Ten years ago it _____

   (not have) convenient public transport.

3. I _____ (not live) here for long. I _____ (move) here three

   years ago.

4. Maybe my town _____ (change) in the future, I _____

   (not really know).

■ Task Five: Vocabulary brainstorm (2)

Another topic which may be covered at this stage is 'Work or Study'.

Brainstorm useful vocabulary and phrases related to your work or study.

■ Task Six: Questions and answers (2)

In pairs, think of four questions about work or study using a range of tenses. The fourth question can be in any tense you like.

Now	
In the past	
In the future	
Your choice	

Now find another partner and take it in turns to ask and answer questions.

This worksheet is based on Part 1 of the IELTS Speaking test.

■ Task One: Vocabulary brainstorm

Brainstorm vocabulary and phrases related to **Photos** and **Free time**.

■ Task Two: Questions and answers

1. Read the questions and carry out the interview in pairs.

   Let's talk about photos now.

   - How often do you take photos? [Why/Why not?]

   - Do you prefer taking photos of people or of places? [Why?]

   - What do you do with the photos you take? [Why/Why not?]

   - Do you think the way people take photos is changing? [Why/Why not?]

   Let's talk about free time now.

   - How much free time do you normally have? [Why/Why not?]

   - What do you like doing best in your free time? [Why?]

   - Have your leisure activities changed much since you were young? [Why/Why not?]

   - If you had more free time, how would you spend it? [Why?]

2. Now watch Inmi and Leonardo do this part of the test on the DVD. Did you manage to answer as fully as they did?

■ Task Three: Watch and listen

1. Watch this part of the DVD again and make notes in the table below and on the next page.

What does Inmi say about …	What does Leonardo say about …
How often she takes photos?	How often he takes photos?
Whether she prefers taking photos of people or places and why?	Whether he prefers taking photos of people or places and why?
What she does with the photos she takes?	What he does with the photos he takes?
Whether the way people take photos is changing?	Whether the way people take photos is changing?
How much free time she normally has?	How much free time he normally has?

What does Inmi say about …	What does Leonardo say about …
What she likes doing best in her free time?	What he likes doing best in his free time?
How she would spend more free time?	Whether his leisure activities have changed much since he was young?

Compare your notes with another student.

2. Watch this part of the DVD again if necessary and discuss these questions:

- Which questions do Inmi and Leonardo answer well?

- Were there any questions they could have answered better?

- Who do you think gave the best answers in this part of the test?

■ Task Four: Focus on language

1. Expressions of liking and disliking

Both Inmi and Leonardo say that they prefer taking photos of people. Look at the following expressions of liking and disliking and decide whether they are followed by the infinitive (with or without 'to') or the gerund ('-ing').

| Like | Would like | Prefer | Would rather |
| Enjoy | Love | Hate | Can't stand |

In pairs, discuss things that you like and dislike using these verbs.

2. Adverbs of frequency

The first question on photos asks **how often** the candidate takes photos, and the first question on free time asks how much free time the candidate **normally** has. In the question on taking photos Leonardo says 'I **usually** take photos when I go on a trip.'

Put the following adverbs of frequency in order starting with the most frequent and ending with the least frequent. Note that some of them have the same meaning.

> sometimes   occasionally   seldom   from time to time   always   rarely
> often   frequently   never   usually

In pairs, discuss what you do at the weekend using these adverbs.

■ Task Five: Talking about a topic

In pairs, write four questions on one of the following topics.

> music   sport   travel   holidays   reading   films   TV   clothes
> spare time   shopping   transport

Now find another partner and ask and answer the questions.

This worksheet is based on Part 2 of the IELTS Speaking test.

■ Task One: Fill the gaps

Below is the introduction that you will be given to this part of the test. Work with a partner and read and complete the gaps with the missing words from the box.

Now, I'm going to give you a _____ and I'd like you to talk about it for one to

_____ minutes. Before you _____, you'll have one minute to

_____ about what you're going to _____. You can make some

_____ if you wish. Do you understand? Here's some _____

and a pencil for _____ notes and here's your topic. I'd like you to

_____ a situation when someone that you didn't know helped you.

describe	making	notes	paper	say	talk	think	topic	two

■ Task Two: Making notes

1. In one minute write brief notes on what you are going to say.

2. Compare your notes with a partner.

■ Task Three: Watch and listen

DVD

1. Watch Inmi do this part of the test and complete the table below.

What the situation was	
When and where it happened	
How the person helped her	
How she felt in that situation	

- How easy does Inmi find it to do this part of the test?

- Do you think that her notes helped her to do the task?

- Did she use the prompts on the card to help her organise the task?

2. Watch Leonardo do this part of the test and complete the table below.

What the situation was	
When and where it happened	
How the person helped him	
How he felt in that situation	

- How easy does Leonardo find it to do this part of the test?

- Do you think his notes helped him to do the task?

- How does he organise the task?

3. Now look again at your notes and consider how helpful they will be for your talk. Add one or two ideas to extend your talk if you need to speak for longer.

■ Task Four: Focus on pronunciation

With a partner, practise reading the following sentences related to the Part 2 topic. Focus on:

- stressing the key words and ideas

- linking words in phrases together

- chunking the words into meaningful groups.

1. To go back home I took a bus with my friend.

2. I knew where I got off, but after getting off the bus I got lost.

3. The more I walked along the street the more difficult it was for me to find my way home.

■ Task Five: Focus on language

Both Inmi and Leonardo attempt to use reported speech in their talks. Put the following direct speech related to Leonardo's talk into reported speech in the past.

1. 'I am lost.'   Example: *He said (that) he was lost.*

2. 'How old are you?'   _____

3. 'What are you doing here?'   _____

4. 'Don't worry. Come with us and we will show you.'   _____

■ Task Six: Talk time

1. Give a two-minute talk to a partner based on your notes and your discussion of the DVD.

2. Listen to your partner's talk and time it for two minutes.

3. Discuss the following questions with your partner:

- How easy did you find the talk?

- Did you find your notes helpful? Why/Why not?

- How did you organise your task?

- How could you extend your task if needed?

This worksheet is designed to give further practice in Part 2 of the IELTS Speaking test.

■ Task One: Language focus – cohesive devices

These are an important aid in structuring your talk.

The following six cohesive devices are useful for sequencing events. Pair each of these with the one with a similar meaning.

After that In the beginning	At first Eventually	In the end Later on

■ Task Two: Making notes

Look at Task Card 2. On the mind map below make notes about this topic. Then compare your notes with a partner.

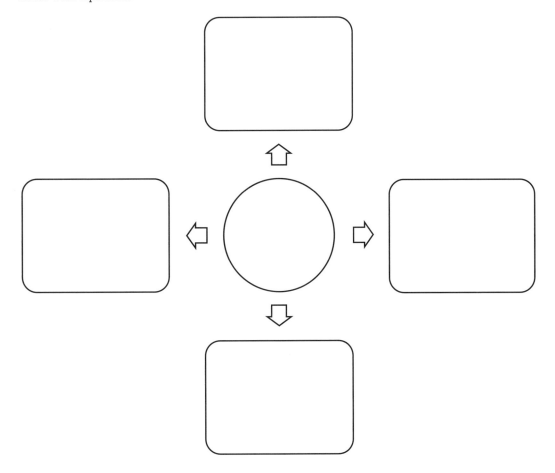

■ Task Three: Talk time

1. Carry out the two-minute talk in turns with your partner. In your talk try to incorporate some of the cohesive devices related to sequencing events.

    While your partner is talking, listen and make notes in the box on the next page to check that they cover all the points in the task.

2. Discuss with your partner how the task was completed and how useful your mind map notes were. Are there any other ways of making notes that you would find more effective?

■ Task Four: Language focus – cohesive devices (2)

These cohesive devices are useful in structuring descriptions or arguments.

Fill in the table with the examples of cohesive devices given below. There are two devices for each function.

Actually	Whereas	Particularly	Basically	To begin with	On the other hand
Specifically	First of all				

Giving the first opinion or fact	
Comparing or contrasting	
Introducing a statement or opinion	
Giving an example or more specific information	

■ Task Five: Making notes (2)

Look at Task Card 3. In the box below make notes about this topic.

■ Task Six: Talk time (2)

1. Carry out the two-minute talk in turns with your partner. In your talk try to incorporate some of the cohesive devices related to structuring discourse.

   While your partner is speaking, listen and make notes in the box below to check that they cover all the points in the task.

2. Discuss with your partner how the task was completed and how useful the preparation notes were.

■ Task Seven: Game – Just a Minute

Look at the words below. Your teacher will explain what you need to do.

1. Music   2. Sport   3. Travel   4. Holidays   5. Reading   6. Films

This worksheet is based on Part 3 of the IELTS Speaking test.

■ Task One: Fill the gaps

DVD

Watch the examiner introduce this part of the test on the DVD and fill in the missing words.

We've been _____ about a situation _____ someone you

didn't _____ helped you, and I'd like _____ (2 words)

with you one or two more _____ questions related to this.

Let's consider _____ of all children _____ others.

■ Task Two: Vocabulary brainstorm

Brainstorm words and phrases related to children helping others.

■ Task Three: Questions and answers

Read the questions below and practise asking and answering them in pairs.

• What kinds of thing can children do to help in the home?

• How can children best learn to be helpful to others?

• In what ways can schools encourage children to help the community?

■ Task Four: Watch and listen

1. Watch Inmi doing this part of the test and complete the following chart.

Things children can do to help in the home	
How children can learn to be helpful to others	
Ways schools can encourage children to help the community	

2. Discuss the following questions with a partner.

• What do you think Inmi does well?

• What do you think she could do better?

• Do you agree with her ideas on children helping others?

3. Watch Leonardo doing this part of the test and complete the following chart.

Things children can do to help in the home	
How children can learn to be helpful to others	
Ways schools can encourage children to help the community	

4. Discuss the following questions with a partner:

- What do you think Leonardo does well?

- What do you think he could do better?

- Do you agree with his ideas on children helping others?

■ Task Five: Focus on language

1. Choose the correct form to complete these sentences.

- Young children/childrens often enjoy to help/helping round the house.

- It depends/It's depend on the age of the children.

- They can learn to be/being helpful through watch/watching others.

- They might be interested of/interested in helping/to help orphans.

- The teacher knows how/that to teach them/they to help others.

- The first thing is being tidy and not throwing/don't throw their things on the floor.

- They must to do/do something for help/to help their parents.

- The first model is/are their parents.

- Show the different things which/what they can do to help.

- That's a bit/rather a difficult question.

2. From the table below match a word from column A with a word or phrase in column B to describe some household tasks.

Note that some verbs, e.g. *tidy up*, can take various options.

A	B
make	the carpet
lay	the washing up
iron	the rubbish
do	the younger children
tidy up	the table
vacuum	the clothes
put out	the grass
cut	the toys
look after	the beds

This worksheet is based on Part 3 of the IELTS Speaking test.

■ Task One: Questions and answers

Read the questions below about working for other people without payment and practise asking and answering them in pairs.

- What types of voluntary work are most popular in your country?

- How do you think individuals might benefit from doing voluntary work?

- In which ways can voluntary work improve life for the community?

■ Task Two: Watch and listen

 DVD ▶

1. Watch Inmi doing this part of the test and complete the following chart.

Popular types of voluntary work in her country	
How individuals might benefit from doing voluntary work	
How voluntary work can improve life for the community	

2. Discuss the following questions with a partner:

- What do you think Inmi does well?

- What do you think she could do better?

- Were her answers on working for other people without payment the same as yours?

DVD ▶

3. Watch Leonardo doing this part of the test and complete the following chart.

Popular types of voluntary work in his country	
The age of people who normally do voluntary work	
How individuals might benefit from doing voluntary work	
How voluntary work can improve life for the community	

4. Discuss the following questions with a partner:

- What do you think Leonardo does well?

- What do you think he could do better?

- Were his answers on working for other people without payment the same as yours?

■ Task Three: Focus on language

1. Leonardo talks about making the community a better place to live in. In each part of the test it is helpful to be able to make comparisons. Complete the following sentences with an appropriate comparative phrase.

- Young people do not do voluntary work _____ as retired people.

- Young people do voluntary work _____ than retired people.

- Older people do voluntary work _____ (frequent) young people.

- Wealthy people do not need nearly _____ (help) poor people.

- Some communities are _____ (good) others.

2. Inmi tries to say that voluntary work can be very *fulfilling*. Adjectives of emotions and feelings usually have two forms, e.g. relaxing, relaxed. Complete the following sentences with the correct form of the adjective.

- Helping others can be very _____ (fulfilling/fulfilled).

- You can feel very _____ (fulfilling/fulfilled) when helping others.

- I was _____ (amazing/amazed) by how much they did to help.

- It is _____ (amazing/amazed) how much they managed to help.

- Some voluntary work can be really _____ (interesting/interested).

- Retired people might be most _____ (interesting/interested) in voluntary work.

■ Task Four: Game – Making Comparisons

In pairs, look back at the list of tasks for helping in the house in Worksheet 5 **Task Five**, Activity 2. Choose two of these tasks and then write five sentences making comparisons between them. Your teacher will tell you what to do.

This worksheet is based on the whole of the IELTS Speaking test.

■ Task One: You are the examiner!

1. You now have the chance to be an IELTS 'examiner'. Read through what the 'examiner' needs to say in each part of the test below. Your teacher will tell you what you need to do.

PART 1 (4–5 minutes)

Let's talk about what you do. Do you work or are you a student?

If the candidate works:

- What kind of work do you do?

- Why did you choose this kind of work?

- Do you prefer working in a team or working alone? [Why/Why not?]

If the candidate studies:

- What subject do you study?

- Why did you choose this subject?

- Do you prefer studying in a group or studying alone? [Why/Why not?]

Now let's talk about sports.

- What is your favourite sport? [Why?]

- How often do you play sports yourself? [Why/Why not?]

- Do you prefer watching sports live or on TV? [Why/Why not?]

- If you had the chance to meet a famous sports person, who would you choose? [Why/Why not?]

PART 2 (3–4 minutes)

Examiner: Now, I'm going to give you a topic and I'd like you to talk about it for one to two minutes. Before you talk, you'll have one minute to think about what you're going to say. You can make some notes if you wish. Do you understand?

Here's some paper and a pencil for making notes (*hand over blank paper and a pencil*) and here's your topic (*hand over topic*).

I'd like you to describe something that you would like to do in the future if you had the chance.

(*At the end of 1 minute's preparation:*)

All right? Can you start speaking now, please?

(*At the end of the 2 minutes, ask the following rounding-off question:*)

Do you like making plans for the future?

Thank you.

PART 3 (4–5 minutes)

Examiner: We've been talking about something that you would like to do in the future if you had the chance, and I'd like to discuss with you one or two more general questions related to this. Let's consider first of all ...

(*Select one or two of the following sets of questions to develop a discussion:*)

- Making plans for the future

  – What kinds of thing do people make plans for in their daily life?

  – Can you think of any reasons why some individuals are better than others at planning?

  – Do you think that important events are always more successful if they have been carefully planned?

- Predicting the future

  – What kinds of thing might people predict about the future?

  – What kinds of situation do businesses need to predict?

  – Do you think there might be any problems in predicting future events?

Examiner: Thank you very much. That is the end of the Speaking test.

2. As you are listening to the 'candidate', make notes in the box below and give feedback at the end of the test.

This worksheet summarises the IELTS Speaking test and reviews the format and tasks.

Now you have watched the DVD and completed Worksheets 1 to 7, you should have a very good idea of the format and tasks in the Speaking test.

■ Task One: Fill the gaps

Fill in the missing information about the Speaking test.

1. The Speaking test lasts for _____ minutes.

2. There are _____ parts to the Speaking test.

3. The format is _____ candidate/s and _____ examiner/s.

4. In Part _____, the examiner asks you about familiar personal topics.

5. In Part 2, the candidate speaks about a topic for _____ minutes.

6. In Part _____, the discussion is more general.

■ Task Two: True or false?

Read the following statements and write 'True' or 'False' next to each one.

1. At the start of the test, the examiner will want to see your passport or identity card.

2. The first set of questions in the test is always about your work or studies.

3. The examiner will enter into a discussion with you in Part 1.

4. In Part 2, you can choose the topic you speak about.

5. In Part 2, you have 2 minutes to prepare before you begin speaking.

6. You can make notes in preparation for your talk in Part 2.

7. In Part 2, after you have finished speaking, the examiner asks you 3 further questions.

8. Part 3 is about a different topic from the one in Part 2.

9. In Part 3, the questions are general and not personal.

Check your answers with a partner and then watch the whole Speaking test on the DVD to see if you were right.

■ Task Three: Marking and assessment

Below are nine pieces of advice for getting good marks in each section of the assessment criteria. Work with a partner and put them in the correct box.

• Use a range of structures.

• Try to develop your ideas logically and fluently.

• Use intonation and stress to help convey meaning.

• Try to use interesting words and phrases, not just the same ones all the time.

• Try to connect your ideas together clearly.

- Try to be precise in the words you use.

- Try not to hesitate for too long before you speak.

- Listen carefully to what you are saying, and correct any mistakes that you hear yourself make.

- Speak clearly and intelligibly.

Assessment criteria	Advice
Fluency and Coherence	
Lexical Resource	
Grammatical Range and Accuracy	
Pronunciation	

■ Task Four: Preparation

How well prepared are you for the exam? Look at the areas in the table below and put a mark from 1–3:

1	I am very confident	2	I need to practise	3	I need to do a lot more work to prepare

	My mark	What I can do to improve
Answering questions about familiar and personal topics in Part 1		
Talking for 2 minutes in Part 2		
Taking part in the general discussion in Part 3		

Discuss with your partner what you can do to improve, and make notes in the table.

NOTES

NOTES

TASK CARD 3

PART 2

Describe a special friend from your schooldays.

You should say:

what the friend is like
how you became friends
what you used to do together

and explain why the friend is so special to you

You will have to talk about the topic for 1 to 2 minutes.

You have 1 minute to think about what you are going to say.

You can make some notes to help you if you wish.

TASK CARD 4

PART 2

Describe something that you would like to do in the future if you had the chance.

You should say:

what you would like to do
when you would like to do it
who you would like to do it with

and explain why you would like to do this

You will have to talk about the topic for 1 to 2 minutes.

You have 1 minute to think about what you are going to say.

You can make some notes to help you if you wish.